HOW TO STAY
TOGETHER

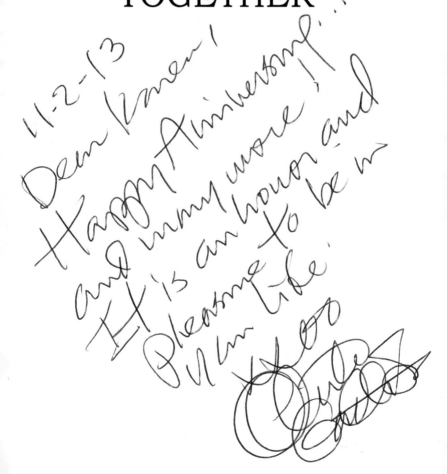

11-2-13

Dear Karen!

Happy Anniversary!...
and many more!!
It is an honor and
Pleasure to be in
your life.

HOW TO STAY TOGETHER

WHETHER YOU WANT TO OR NOT

DR. ANITA GADHIA-SMITH

iUniverse LLC
Bloomington

How To Stay Together
Whether You Want To Or Not

iUniverse books may be ordered through booksellers or by contacting:

iUniverse LLC
1663 Liberty Drive
Bloomington, IN 47403
www.iuniverse.com
1-800-Authors (1-800-288-4677)

ISBN: 978-1-4917-0818-7 (sc)
ISBN: 978-1-4917-0819-4 (ebk)

Printed in the United States of America.

iUniverse rev. date: 09/20/2013

CONTENTS

THIS BOOK IS DEDICATED
TO MY HUSBAND:

RONALD E. SMITH, MD, PHD
CAPTAIN, MEDICAL CORPS,
UNITED STATES NAVY

(THE LAST AMERICAN HERO)

FOREWORD

This new book by Dr. Anita Gadhia-Smith is a true teaching tool on relationships. It covers the complex element of the human experience from every angle and opens our eyes to issues we have never even considered. It is written in a very positive and fluid style, which makes one eager to move from one chapter to the next, realizing that one can learn from every step of the book.

Dr. Anita is an experienced relationship therapist, and this is shown by her extraordinary insight on how to face and deal with inter-personal problems. She offers advice to redirect relationships that have gone wrong, and she gives us valuable guidelines for making good relationships even better. She delves deep into our souls and helps us realize that even if something has gone wrong in a relationship, one can reroute it to find great comfort and happiness.

This book makes you aware that you have to be actively involved in making a meaningful life with your partner, and that it is up to you to create a loving and positive environment. Taking on this challenge personally, every day, will lead to a successful life together.

Dr. Anita has done it again. This is a 'good read' with an incredible amount of clinical and practical advice for both the general public and her professional mental health colleagues. She demonstrates why she is such a good therapist. We all will learn a great deal from this book.

Inge Guen, PsyD

INTRODUCTION

After 15 years of marriage and 51 years of life, I knew it was time to write this book. I married at the age of 36, have weathered many storms in my own marriage and have learned a tremendous amount that I want to share. I am a psychotherapist who specializes in relationship issues, as well as addiction issues, and have been working with individuals, couples, and families in my practice for fifteen years. I have extensive clinical training as well as first-hand experience in working with a vast array of relationship issues.

My own marriage was extremely difficult in the beginning. Actually, that is an understatement. It was a nightmare. The amount, intensity, and frequency of unmanageable conflict were beyond my comprehension when I decided to marry. I had no idea what I was doing, and I am eternally grateful to my family, therapist, and friends who got me through those rough times. I had no clue that I was not good relationship material at the time of my marriage. I was self-centered, immature, and severely lacking in relationship skills. I have learned that the best way to learn how to do something is to actually do it. For me, this meant staying in a relationship long enough to learn how to have a good one.

After exhausting myself by blaming my husband for several years and getting nowhere, I finally began to look at myself. This was the missing piece that unlocked the door to true progress and growth. I learned that there was much that I could not readily see about myself that I later came to understand after persevering in a sustained effort to grow. I learned about the meaning of love and how to put it into action.

In my practice as a psychotherapist, I see many people give up on their relationships too quickly. This, in turn, affects their other relationships, their children, and society as a whole. We have become a disposable culture, ready to throw out what we have all too quickly in the hopes of finding something better. We are often lazy and entitled when it comes to getting what we want, when we want it, the way we want it.

Many people want the other person to change but are slow to recognize their own shortcomings. This is very difficult to do on your own, but with help, can become a life-transforming practice. I was definitely in this category. I knew how to leave, but I did not know how to stay. I had to learn how to stay, as well as how to enjoy it!

If you are thinking of leaving a relationship, my message is to stay and work on yourself before you leave. Otherwise, you run the risk of just taking yourself with you wherever you go. It is much easier to leave than to stay, but with some effort, you may find that you already have what you wanted all along.

A healthy relationship is one of the most significant predictors of life satisfaction, health, longevity, and happiness. May you grow to love your relationship more and more each and every day . . .

Dr. Anita Gadhia-Smith
Practicaltherapy.net

1

COURTSHIP

Are you challenged by relationships? If so, this book is for you. Relationships are by far the most worthwhile but most difficult part of life. We are transformed by our relationships. One relationship can change the course of your life forever. And it can all start in the blink of an eye, when you least expect it.

Meeting someone new can be a very daunting task. Try to be clear about what kind of relationship you really want. You can become the type of person that you would want to attract by embodying the very characteristics that you seek in a partner. Cultivate interests and activities that you would want to share with someone special. When you meet someone that you are interested in, let him take the lead if you are a female, and take the lead if you are a male. For same-sex relationships, choose what is most comfortable for you. Let yourself get to know the person at a natural pace, and have a good time.

When we begin a new relationship, we enter into the courtship phase. During this time, we show our best self to the other person. We do a courtship dance together to see if we are a fit. Our masks are intact, our game face is on, and we keep things light and fun. We want to make a good impression so that we are desired by the other. We invest time and energy in getting to know the other person to see if we want to continue the relationship and possibly go deeper.

During courtship, we progress from getting to know one another to attachment, and then to possibly to falling in love. This can happen quickly or slowly, depending on your capacity for attachment, intimacy, and readiness to partner up. I do not recommend having sex while you are casually dating. Once you have both decided to be exclusive, then it is time to go ahead and explore each other sexually. There are no rules about how long courtship should last, but it is generally wise to wait at least six months before making a commitment. The courtship phase of a relationship can be swift and exciting, gentle and slow, confusing, frightening, and even addictive.

Courtship can span a wide range of forms regardless of age or life experience. Sometimes for younger people, courtship can take several years, as a sense of self has not yet been fully formed, and discernment about what really fits us is still unclear. I have also seen older couples partner fairly quickly, as they both know what they are looking for and do not hesitate to jump in when they find it. Later in life, we also feel a keener awareness of the passage of time and do not wish to waste our time and pass up opportunities.

The critical thing during the courtship phase is to discern whether the person you are dating is a good match and whether they are truly available to you. A person who is available may not be perfect or have every quality that you seek, but if there is a willingness to work on issues together, then you have a good potential partner. Sometimes someone may appear to be available, but once you get into a relationship with them, you find that you can only get so close or that they are unwilling to do the work to try to grow. Does this person really want a relationship and have what it takes to evolve together as a couple? If not, then don't waste your time. That is a good time to leave.

If you have a history of being attracted to unavailable people, you might repeatedly find yourself in situations where your needs are not met. This could stem from having had an unavailable parent early in life, or many other life experiences. Individual psychotherapy can take you a long way towards understanding your history, psyche, and behavior patterns. If you find yourself repeating the same behavior again and again and not knowing how you did it one more time, seek help to untangle your knots. Through therapy, you can learn not only what drives you but also how to change your patterns. You can achieve a breakthrough.

Once you have met a person that you are interested in, you may ask yourself what is the best way to get to know him or her. The world has been changed significantly by the advent of technology over the last couple of decades. It used to be that the only way to get to know someone was to go out on a date and sit face-to-face. Now we have a multitude of options, including telephone, e-mail, Skype, text messages, and social networking sites, just to name a few. Many people begin their long-term relationships as the result of meeting online or through a dating site.

While technology makes it possible to gain initial access to more people than ever before, we still only really get to know someone when we spend time with them in person. The dying art of human connection through actual face-to-face interactions is still the most reliable method of building a relationship with someone. While you may use technology to get started, use actual personal interaction to build the relationship as much as possible. You need access to all five senses in order to build a solid foundation with someone. Going on vacation together is an excellent way to determine whether you are suited to spend real time together and take the relationship to the next level.

Intuition can also play an important role in the courtship phase. Sometimes we are innately drawn to someone and do not understand why. This may not be the type of person we think we would be attracted to. The opposite can also occur. We can also be intuitively turned off by someone for no apparent reason. There are some things that we cannot figure out in our rational minds. However, our unconscious never sleeps; it is always working and can guide us in an uncanny way. Keep yourself in fit emotional, physical, and spiritual condition so that you can trust your intuition. Sometimes, it can be our best friend.

If a relationship doesn't work out, move on. There is no reason to hang on to something that is never going to work. Your time is the most precious commodity that you have. You can always earn more money, but you can never get back lost time. Treasure your time, and use it wisely. Invest yourself in people, places, and situations that also invest in you. This means that you engage in relationships where there is mutuality, and avoid those that are one-sided. A common scenario in the courtship phase is when you meet someone, think you like them, and then start to wonder whether or not they like you. Then you try to read the signals. Should I continue to call the person even if they haven't called me? And the most commonly obsessed-over question of all: "What does it mean that he/she hasn't called me?" If there is mutuality in the relationship, you will not wonder if the person likes you. You will know.

Some courtships are meant just for practice. We are being taught something about ourselves or about other people, and the person we are dating is our teacher. Always try to learn from every experience, and you will be more in tune with yourself and your needs the next time around. Don't be afraid to practice. We are supposed to practice everything we do in life until we are advanced enough to move on to the next level.

Always try to keep an open mind. You never know who God has in store for you. Throw away your model of exactly who your partner should be and what they should look like. Age and looks really do not matter all that much anyway. They both change over time. Have you ever gotten to know someone, and then realized that the way they look to you is completely different than when you first met them? That is because once you know someone, your perception of them changes.

We grew up thinking that the right person would come into our lives and make it all okay. It was just supposed to happen spontaneously. We thought that this was the way life worked. We had a fantasy of the "perfect one" who would understand us, automatically know what we wanted, and anticipate our needs. Then that person would try to win us over by fulfilling all of those needs. This would be the person that would complete our world. And then we could live happily ever after . . .

Why do we fall in love? Falling in love is an obsession that causes us to lose our heads. Is this really what is needed for us to become happy and whole? Nature seems to use some very powerful tricks to get us together with someone and to procreate in order to propagate the species. First, there is the mental obsession with the other person. Then there is the biochemical addiction; your body actually releases chemicals that get you high and keep you in a state of wanting more and more of the other person. You get a release of the addictive hormones when you are with the one you love. It is very powerful and very binding. And it surely keeps you coming back.

What is interesting is that we fall in love even when we do not want to procreate. More and more people today are choosing to be childfree, yet they still want love and partnership. It is a basic, fundamental need to be in partnership with another person. Humans were not meant to be solitary creatures. Our health is better, we live longer happier lives, and we can contribute more to the world as the result of the love we share with a partner. We fall in love in order to bond, but we stay together in order to grow, flourish, and contribute to the world.

During the initial phase of your relationship, give each other plenty of breathing room. Give each other space to grow into the relationship. If this person is meant to be your partner, there is nothing you can do to make it happen, nor is there anything you can do to stop it from happening. Let it happen at its own pace, in its own way, and in God's time.

2

AMBIVALENCE

Ambivalence is a part of all human relationships. It means that different parts of you want two opposing things at the same time. Part of you wants a relationship, and part of you still wants to be single. This seems impossible; you wanted a stable relationship for so long. Now that you have it, you're not sure you want it anymore. How can this be? You ask yourself, "Am I crazy?" You are not crazy. You are just like everybody else.

Human beings often have opposing desires that are mutually exclusive. This can stem from unresolved internal conflicts having to do with attachment, intimacy, separation, and authenticity. Ambivalence is a normal part of the process leading up to commitment, and can even persist for many years into a relationship. Expect it, allow it, and take the time to work through it.

One of the most important aspects of addressing and resolving your own ambivalence is to allow and express both sides of it. We need to be very selective about where, how, and when we express the negative feelings, but they must be permitted. We often find it difficult to allow ourselves to own feelings that we consider to be inappropriate in a given situation.

Depending on our value system, we may feel that it is okay to express loving feelings but forbidden to express anger, guilt, shame, dislike, and hatred. Remember that where there is love, there is often hate. You can't have one without the other, even if the hatred is repressed. The opposite of love is not hate; it is indifference. It is indifference, not anger, that kills a relationship.

Repressing the negative feelings only makes them intensify, and prolongs the ambivalence. By bringing all of our feelings out into the light of day, we can allow both extremes, express the feelings, and then decide what we want to do about it. We can then make a healthy choice for ourselves. Being able to act in your own best interest despite having ambivalence is a sign of emotional maturity and mental health.

Another aspect of a long-term relationship that is related to ambivalence is the tendency to fall in and out of love. If you are single, this could occur with different partners, but if you are in a relationship, it can happen repeatedly with the same person. If you stay in the relationship, work through the conflicts, and don't get involved with someone else, you can fall back in love with your partner. Each time you fall back in love, you fall more deeply into the love and intimacy.

This is how a relationship strengthens over time. The progression is not linear. It is more like a two steps forward, one step back process. Each time you recommit and move forward again, your relationship grows. The richness of this experience is incomparable to the cyclical nature falling in love with different people. With different people, you only get so far each time. There is less depth to the relationships, because they only get to a certain developmental point, and then stop. If you find yourself in a repeating cycle of changing names and faces at a certain point in your relationships, you may be blocked. I would recommend that you seek counseling in order to break through the barrier that keeps you from sustaining and deepening intimacy in your life.

Sometimes, ambivalence can set in at a later stage of a committed relationship. At midlife, many people struggle, both consciously and unconsciously, with what has been done and what has been left undone in their lives. When we wake up to the reality of our mortality at midlife, we realize that we don't want to miss anything before our life ends. There can be a gradual or sudden shift in consciousness that changes our universe. We take stock of where we are, and also grieve the paths not taken.

This can lead to a questioning of our choices and the realization that time is too short. We only have so much time left, and if there is something that we have never allowed ourselves to do, we may want to do it. This unexpressed desire may be in direct conflict with our relationship. It can sometimes manifest as wanting to leave a relationship or by having an affair in order to experience something different. If we can find a way to recognize and express our unmet needs and desires without blowing up our life, we can sustain the stability of our relationship and also resolve the midlife issues.

In my psychotherapy practice, I have seen many patients who have been in long-term committed relationships, and who still struggle with their ambivalence about the relationship many years into it. It can take quite a while to resolve ambivalence. Sometimes, the ambivalence never gets completely resolved, but people learn to live with it. It is possible to accept the ambivalence as part of life, focus on what is good, and live full and contented lives anyway.

We don't always have to resolve everything in order to be happy. If you are supposed to stay in the relationship, you will never really take the steps to leave. You may think about it a lot, but an invisible unseen force will keep you there. It just may be because you are still supposed to be there.

3

RESPONSIBILITY

One of the hallmarks of growth in adulthood and self-actualization is learning to take responsibility for our own lives. This is truly one of the keys to personal happiness and fulfillment, whether you are in a relationship or not. A problematic pattern that often arises for people who are in difficult relationships is that they tend to hold the other person responsible for their happiness. Most of the time, they do not even realize that they are doing it.

This relational pattern can stem from dysfunctional family belief systems, faulty societal messages, and unrealistic fantasy. Our families-of-origin play the key role in setting our psychological hard drives. If we saw dysfunctional parents play out a particular scenario, we may play out the same roles in our own lives on autopilot. It may be all we know and understand. It can be difficult to conceive of another way of doing things until you know what else is possible.

Many young people have grown up watching movies that portray the love of his or her life as a hero who will magically appear and rescue them from the difficulties of the world. The message is that your true love will make it all okay. Just look good enough, be an attractive enough package, and you will attract "The One." One of the problems with this is that we spend more time trying to look our best than to actually be the best person we can be. Ultimately, it is not about finding the right person; it is about becoming the right person. That is an inside job. Once you become your best self, you will attract higher quality relationships, and the relationship you already have will up-level to a higher plane.

Another issue at play in today's world is the increasingly pervasive tendency to put the focus on looking good, rather than actually becoming a person of substance. In our culture, we spend vast sums of money purchasing all of the things that we are being told we must have in order to be acceptable and successful. For women particularly, this can mean expensive packaging designed to attract a similarly expensively packaged provider and partner with whom the perfect life will be created.

In many cases, this means having the right friends and things, living in the right neighborhoods, driving the right cars, and sending your kids to the right schools. I have seen many couples who seemed to have it all on the outside barely be able to have a meaningful conversation with each other. If the solution is to always fix the outsides without ever really examining the insides, the tendency is to then focus on changing your partner rather than yourself. After all, your partner is the closest thing within reach on the outside.

People spend countless amounts of time and energy trying to get someone else to change and to do what they want them to do. I cannot think of a bigger waste of time than trying to change someone else. The more you try to change another person to suit yourself, the more they will resent you. People do change, but they have to want to do it for themselves, and they have to be ready to do the work to get there. We can barely change ourselves, let alone other people. Yet this is the default coping strategy for many people who sense a problem in their relationship.

The results of placing this burden on your partner include chronic disappointment, hurt, isolation, anger, shame, guilt, low self-esteem, intense conflict, and feeling like a victim. One of the primary methods that we use to express our need for change is by complaining. Don't complain. Instead of complaining, do something to improve yourself, your attitude, or your own life. If you try to improve yourself instead of your partner, you will feel better regardless of whether your partner changes or not. My experience has been that as one person begins to change him—or herself for the better and leaves their partner alone, the other partner starts to notice and will often follow along in making constructive changes.

If you had a parent who overindulged you, the passive tendency can be difficult to overcome. When you grow up with a model of life that others are there to please you or cater to your needs, you remain a child. You develop unrealistic expectations of others and unconsciously expect others to treat you the way that your parents did. It stifles the drive energy to go out into the world and do something. We all have a gift to give the world, and it is our purpose in life to find out what it is and then to go out and do it.

Another variation of this issue is might occur if you had parents who were not there for you. This can set you up to unconsciously seek out partners to parent you to make up for the deficits of your childhood. This dynamic is fraught with difficulty, especially if your partner ever happens to fall short, which even the best partners do. Then your repressed painful feelings from childhood can come roaring out at your unsuspecting partner, who had no idea what they were signing up for. Unresolved historical issues can breed hysterical feelings in the present. You will not understand why the rage is so intense, as it is often disproportionate to the current situation when a hidden landmine has been accidentally set off.

In psychological maturity, we learn to be responsible for ourselves within a relationship. First we learn to be together. Then we must face and resolve our unmet dependency issues from childhood, and choose responsibility. We must give up unrealistic expectations of our partner, and learn to soothe ourselves, build basic trust, and take responsibility for our own happiness. We must learn to be by ourselves and be in the relationship without losing ourselves. This is one of the most crucial developmental tasks in both childhood and adulthood.

It only takes one person to change a relationship. You do not have to wait for your partner to change in order for the relationship to change. If you begin by changing yourself, the relationship will naturally change. This is due to the fact that the dynamics will shift when one of the pieces changes form, because the pieces of the puzzle will no longer fit according to the old model. The good news is that you do have control over your own choices.

Self-care is key. Put this first, and you will have more to give and be more pleasant to be with. It is especially important to focus on getting enough sleep, rest, exercise, optimal nutrition, social support, psychological help, and spiritual direction. It is not selfish to attend to your own needs; it fosters happiness for everyone. It is freeing for you and for all the people who love you. When you release others from the burden of always feeling like they have to please you, everyone can relax and just be themselves. It is no one else's job to make you happy. That is your own responsibility.

You are responsible to create meaning in your life. You cannot make your primary relationship be the sole meaning of your life, but you can create meaning as the result of being in a relationship. When you are in a stable relationship, you have an anchor.

Your energy is not diverted in a multitude of directions towards medicating your loneliness. This can take up huge amounts of time and energy that can be used for something more meaningful.

4

COMMITMENT

Making a commitment to someone is a major developmental step in a relationship. Even though it can be the fruition of your dreams, it can also be terrifying. For some people it is very clear that commitment is the next right thing, but for others doubt can linger even though they feel the desire to commit. I suggest implementing the 80/20 Rule. You do not need to have one hundred percent certainty in order to move forward, but I recommend that you be at least eighty percent sure. In general, if you have eighty percent of what you want, the other twenty percent will work itself out. Eighty percent is enough to go ahead and make the commitment.

Many people see commitment as marked by a particular arrangement, ceremony, or legal agreement. While this is true in the formal sense, commitment is an ongoing process. It does not happen on one particular day. Commitment happens over many years, as we share life experiences with someone, work through our conflicts, and continue to make the decision again and again to stay in the relationship. As time goes on, you become more and more committed to the relationship due to the ongoing investment of your time, energy and money.

Sometimes, one person may not be ready to make a commitment. We all need to play with others for a time in our lives. If someone has not made a commitment to you after two years of dating, they may need to play some more and live out their adolescence. This does not mean that they are a bad person; it just means that they are not developmentally where you are. If you are with someone who is at a much younger developmental point, it is reasonable to move on. If possible, get your playtime out of your system before making a commitment to someone. If it is too late for that, learn how to play without blowing up your life.

At a certain stage in a long-term relationship, someone will step forward and make a move. This could mean a proposal to live together, or maybe a proposal for marriage. Either way, you come to a point of decision. This is it. You are either going to go down a long road together or not. It may or may not work out. Are you willing to take a chance? Even though you can never really be sure of anyone or anything, you have enough data and experience to feel reasonably hopeful that this will work, so you decide to commit. You jump in and hope that it does.

Can we ever really be sure of anyone? No. But we can be sure of ourselves. This means that we each have the internal resources to get ourselves through whatever will happen with the future. Most of us have much more resiliency than we think. And we also have God; He will do whatever we cannot do for ourselves. Between ourselves and God, there is nothing we cannot deal with. There is a time to get off of the sidelines of life, jump in, and take a chance. This is what distinguishes the extraordinary life from the mediocre life.

We can also commit to do everything humanly possible to do our part in the relationship. This means working on our own issues even after we think we are done. It never really ends. If we make the commitment to give it one hundred percent, and stay even when we want to run, we will discover that we are capable of much more than we imagine.

Making a commitment to a relationship means making a commitment to the relationship itself, not just to the other person. The most successful long-term relationships are those where the partners have a strong value commitment to being in a relationship. For example, in arranged marriages in Eastern cultures, partners decide to marry based on shared values and family systems, and then they learn to love one another. They commit first and then learn to love. In Western cultures, we try to learn to love and then we commit. Given that our relationship failure rate is much higher, perhaps we need to focus on becoming the right person and learning to love instead of finding the right person.

Before making a commitment, it is important assess your relationship on many levels. You need to be compatible emotionally, physically, spiritually, and share core family values. It is also advisable to discuss what your vision of an ideal relationship looks like. You want to make sure that the basics are in place before you jump in. Once you assess the potential of the relationship and feel reasonably comfortable with your chances of making it, go for it.

When you make a commitment, it is essential to get both feet into the relationship. Close yourself off to other potential partners but not to other healthy relationships. If you have lingering feelings for a former love, work them out and move on. It will only torture you and your partner if you have unresolved emotional baggage from a past relationship. Seek a therapist or trusted advisor to help you to resolve the past.

You need your whole heart, mind, body, and spirit in your current relationship in order for it to thrive. Be present with your whole self, and give all of yourself to your partner. Even if you are afraid and do not have faith, live as though you do. Give your best to your relationship, and watch it flourish. Live your relationship and your life to the fullest.

5

CONFLICT

Many of us grow up with the expectation that when we meet "the one," we will always love that person forever, and it will just get better and better on its own. The last part is true, if you work on your relationship. But the first part is a little bit more complicated.

After the initial intense phases of falling in love, commitment, and the resolution of ambivalence, there can be an ongoing cycle of falling in love, experiencing conflict, falling out of love, then falling back in love again at an even deeper level. Sometimes the cycles can be lengthy. So long, in fact, that you think the relationship has changed permanently. Perhaps it has, or perhaps you are in one of the inevitable cycles of falling in and out of love.

This is one area that can really take a lot of work to manage. People have different styles of handling conflict. Some are aggressive. You know what they want; they are not afraid to speak up in order to win an argument. Others are passive; they agree compliantly with anything in order to keep the peace. Stuffing feelings can be extremely dangerous. Still others are passive-aggressive, agreeing to your face, but then acting out the conflict sideways. Ultimately, we want to learn to handle conflict assertively, so that we respect both ourselves and others. This means being honest, direct, clear, and mature enough to realize that we all have right to express ourselves and must all compromise in some areas of life.

When you do find yourself engaged in a conflict, it is very useful to employ guidelines for "fair fighting." Some of these guidelines may include: focusing on expressing your own feelings instead of on what the other person did to hurt you; allowing your anger as well as the other person's anger to get out; learning the art of compromise and negotiation; giving yourself and your partner time and space to cool off; and sticking to the subject at hand. The time of conflict is not the time to throw in every grievance you have ever had. You will only get tangled up even more. Try not to be mean. Say what you mean without being mean. Express yourself, but also listen as much as you speak. Finally, follow up with action.

Withdrawing and going on the offensive are two of the most common destructive conflict management tactics. Through withdrawal, we try to cut ourselves off from the problem, hoping that it will go away. We may also be trying to seek revenge or punish through our absence. Going on the offensive is another maladaptive coping mechanism in a conflict situation. It allows the aggressor to try to intimidate the other person in order to win the war. Neither one of these coping mechanisms is very productive, as each leaves an imbalance in the relationship. In order for a conflict to be resolved constructively, both sides need a voice as well as understanding from the other side. Intimidation and avoidance are not winning strategies to keep your love as the top priority.

It is important to keep your romantic love intact and aim for a win-win strategy. Negotiating in a pleasant and respectful manner so that both of you can win is key. Both you and your partner have important perspectives on every issue. If both of you value each other's feelings and opinions, there is a greater likelihood that you will come to a resolution that makes you both feel understood and valued by each other. Ultimately, a constructive solution will provide some of what both of you want, and no one will feel deprived.

Conflicts over priorities and time management, parenting, money, and sex are the most common areas of conflict for couples. It is important that both of you prioritize time for each other for meaningful conversation, sex, fun, and sharing responsibilities. When both of you feel good about the time that is being given to the relationship, you will both feel supported by one another and feel that you are partners working on the same team.

It is important not to brush truly important issues under the rug. If either one of you feels that a problem is important, it must be resolved. It must be repeatedly brought up, discussed, attended to, and resolved until both of you truly feel you have reached a constructive agreement. Agreements can be revisited if they need revision or are not working well for both of you.

Speaking with friends and relatives about your relationship conflict can create additional complications. Since they are not impartial, you may not get neutral feedback. In addition, after your conflict has resolved, they may unknowingly acquire a bias against your partner. While we all need to vent our frustrations, I encourage you to be very discerning about who you talk to about your relationship. This is one of the primary reasons to seek professional help. It is private, confidential, and unbiased. And you will never have to explain to your friends why you ended up staying in a relationship with someone who hurt you so much.

The fact is we all hurt in our relationships. There are few passionate intimate relationships that do not also involve pain and conflict. Where there is little conflict, there is also little passion. And where there is little passion, people tend to lose interest after a time. In my opinion, it is better to have a passionate relationship with conflict than to have a lack of passionate connection and no conflict. We need connection and passion in our lives in order to fully live. We are supposed to experience the full range of human emotions in our relationships, not just the pleasant ones. It is through experiencing and learning to manage all of our emotions that we evolve and mature.

There are certain types of issues that can be deal-breakers in relationships. Violence, chronic infidelity, and addictions are the most common. Deal-breakers can ultimately end your relationship if they are not addressed. However, through appropriate treatment, even the most damaging issues can heal. If the person is willing to seek help, these conditions can be managed, but if not, you have to make a choice that is in your own best interest.

In the case of violence, a victim must walk away from a relationship if safety is at risk. However, there are some situations in which violence can be addressed if anger management treatment is successful. Through appropriate and sustained treatment, aggressive, intimidating, and even violent behavior can be managed and extinguished. When substance abuse and addictions tie in with domestic violence, the first order of business is to address the substance abuse. Once the substances are out of the picture, secondary issues often lessen or disappear completely.

If a person is addicted to mood-altering substances or engaged in any number of other addictive compulsions, they can seek treatment to arrest the addiction and then work on the underlying issues that led them to addiction in the first place. Addiction is one of the most widespread but highly treatable chronic conditions of our time. In today's world, worldwide help is readily available through individual psychotherapy with addiction specialists, 12-step groups, and treatment centers. The most difficult part of treating an addiction is for the addicted person to "hit bottom" and become truly receptive to seeking help and doing the ongoing work in order to sustain change. Once this occurs, lasting and remarkable recovery is possible.

Infidelity is another one of the most common issues that lead to couples living on the brink of splitting up. While infidelity is a highly painful and volatile situation, it can also lead to increased healing and growth in a relationship if both people are willing to work through the underlying relationship issues together and forgive. I have seen many couples recover their marriages after infidelity.

Infidelity can wake up partners to the realization that they have gone to sleep in their relationship and have not attended to their own or to one another's needs. If one person experiences profound deprivation in the relationship, there is fertile ground for acting out. If the infidelity becomes known, there is no choice for partners except to either walk away or confront each other and discover how they got to such a level of distress that infidelity became an option. In other cases, infidelity remains a secret, but the unfaithful partner eventually realizes that they really do want their long-term relationship. Sometimes, experiencing someone else can make you realize that what you already have is what you really want.

If you have been the victim of a partner's infidelity, there are steps you can take to recover. Turn to sources of refuge, such as friends, family, counselors, and God for comfort and support. Seek peace for yourself rather than trying to get all of the answers. There may be some questions that you will never be able to answer. Give yourself extra self-care, rest, treats, and breaks. Let go of your old model of the relationship.

If you stay in your relationship, you will now need a new paradigm for your life. Be creative and reassess your priorities. Make sure that you are spending your time, energy, and money in ways that align with your true values. Forgive the person who has hurt you. Rather than holding on to resentment and becoming bitter, try to forgive and move on so that you will be set free from negative emotions stemming from the past. Finally, trust that good will come out of the situation if you seek it. At a minimum, you will be able to help others who have experienced the same pain.

If the deal-breakers cannot be resolved, a relationship will often come to an end. The three natural outcomes of living in an unmanageable situation are to go crazy, kill yourself, or to disassociate. Of the three, disassociating is the healthiest option. Some people do this by checking out of the relationship while staying in it, by being there without really being there. Others find compulsive diversions and addictions of their own. Some of these include work, church, hobbies, other relationships, electronics, and addictive substances. Still others find it necessary to leave the relationship for their survival.

Family of origin issues can reincarnate in our romantic relationships. If you are recreating your ancient childhood dramas with your partner, you may be playing out an old dynamic from the past. Whatever you saw your parents do or not do has a huge impact on your relationship hard drive. It can also lead to acting out unresolved anger with a parent or sibling on your current partner. We sometimes reenact our old family dramas in order to resolve them. Therapy can be very helpful in bringing awareness to our unconscious behaviors.

Once we make the unconscious conscious, we are much less likely to act out the past. We can begin to make new and different choices based on insight and understanding about why we are who we are. We can also learn to communicate through words instead of actions. What we cannot verbalize, we tend to act out through our behavior. Through new communication skills, we can negotiate and grow through our conflicts and get unstuck.

One of the most simple yet powerful communication skills a person can cultivate is being respectful. Much conflict can be avoided by being courteous and cordial. It is very difficult to get angry with someone who is treating you with courtesy and respect, even if you do not like what they are saying. This is accomplished through tone of voice, word choice, and maintaining a loving spirit. You can say almost anything to a person if it is said with love.

Another way to avoid a conflict is to learn to hold your tongue. You will never regret what you did not say. Once something is said, you cannot take it back. Criticism is one of the primary instigators of conflict and defensiveness. It is amazing how many of us have developed a critical spirit without even realizing it. There is a difference between being discerning and being critical. There is an air of negativity around critical people that brings everyone around them down just a notch.

If you receive a valid criticism, try to keep an open mind, examine where there is truth, and take the teaching. Defensiveness will just keep a conflict going. It might be wiser to just say, "Hmm, you may have a point; let me give that some thought," and then move on. Try to keep yourself calm in the craziness.

Then reflect on the substance of what was presented to you and use what is helpful for you to improve yourself. Even though you may not like the form, the substance of what is being said may be valuable for you. The people who are closest to us see us beneath the exterior that we present to the outside world. They are in a position to tell us the truth, and we can be grateful for that.

Communication is a critical component of dealing with relationships. Try to make an effort to communicate something of value, not just to talk at your partner. This means honestly sharing your feelings, desires, and needs. If you keep the focus of your words on your own feelings, your partner will be more likely to hear your message without feeling defensive.

Tone is also very important in communication. It reveals your spirit even more than the actual words that you use. People will respond much more to your spirit and energy than they will to the words you say. Regardless of what you say, the most important thing to communicate is your love for the other person. If he or she feels your love, the exchange will bring you closer together.

There may be times when your partner is just not receptive to talking. Leave your partner alone when he needs space and wait until it is a better time to talk. Trying to force people to talk before they are ready to do so often results in an altercation. We cannot selfishly force our will upon others. If there is a particular issue that your partner is not yet ready to face, try to take some time to get there together. We need patience as well as perseverance in moving towards our goals.

Although we need to try to continue to address significant unresolved issues until we have worked them through, most couples have some issues that will never be fully resolved. This is a fact of life that can be difficult to accept. Partial fulfillment and progress towards resolution can be enough to keep us in the relationship, motivated, and moving in the right direction. With chronic issues that persist, we will have more peace if we continue to work on them, even if we only work on our own side of the issue. It is empowering to change our own attitudes and actions, even if no one else does.

Be mindful of your words. People will generally become what you tell them they are. If you affirm their good qualities, they are more likely to behave well. If you tell someone that they are a kind and loving person, they are more likely to behave that way. You can set yourself up by your own suggestions. If you criticize someone's faults, they are more likely to behave badly. We all can think of examples from our childhoods of things that our parents told us that we embraced with undying belief.

When you are at an impasse in a conflict, try to take the high road. This means taking the first step towards your partner. If you have a resistant or stubborn partner, stay steady and persevere. Keep throwing out love, no matter what, for as long as it takes. Love is far more powerful than anger or stonewalling.

It is ultimately the most powerful force in the world. It can break down walls because it is irresistible. Be the first one to make up. This is how to win the war.

Once you make up, then it is time to begin to talk and sort out the issues. The starting point is to find your common ground. When you begin by focusing on where you both agree and on what you both want in common, you remember that you are not enemies; you are on the same team. It is very easy to see your partner as an adversary. Most of the time, they are doing the best they can. They have their faults, just like you have yours.

Be the change you want to see. If you really want change, take the lead and work on changing yourself for the better. By working on changing your own destructive patterns, your relationship will change. If you want more respect, practice being respectful. If you want more love, practice being more loving. Your partner is likely to reflect back to you the attitudes and behaviors that you manifest.

When both people consistently work on their own individual side of the equation, profound and lasting change can occur. You will experience a transformation in your relationship that you never imagined possible. People do change. That is, if they want to change and are willing to do the work to get there. There are very few situations that are beyond hope and help.

It is important to be able to distinguish an issue that is truly important from one that is merely irritating. We often ignore serious issues yet behave as though irritations are big problems. For example, if your partner leaves dirty dishes in the sink, it may be irritating, but it is not necessarily a sign that you are disrespected in the relationship. Keep the big picture view of your partnership. As long as the good outweighs the bad, you are ahead of the game. Choose your battles wisely, and try to overlook minor imperfections.

When dealing with a burning issue, it can sometimes be easy to confuse the issue with the person. People have behaviors, but they are not their behaviors. You can love the person even though you do not love what they do. Try to separate the person from their actions. When working through a conflict, focus on the issue at hand, and not on the person as a human being. You are with your partner because you chose this person and you love them. You can still love one another even though you are angry. Always love the person even if you don't love their behavior.

While we all experience challenges in our relationships, our problems do not have to define us or our relationships. It is important to keep a proper perspective and continue to enjoy what adds value to your life. Sometimes we can forget just how much we have to be grateful for. There is a time to set aside your battles and just live.

6

EROS

Sex is what distinguishes a love affair from a friendship. It is a powerful bonding force between partners, relieves stress, is fun, and greatly strengthens a relationship. Chemistry is hard to predict. You cannot create it or keep it down. We can have emotional love and romantic feelings for someone at a deep level, but an emotional relationship is not the same thing as a sexual relationship. As human beings, we are hard wired to need sex, just as we need food and air. Unlike food and air, we can continue to survive if we don't have sex, but the urge towards eros drives our being towards fulfillment at both the unconscious and conscious levels.

The primary desire of a woman is to be desired. Women do much of what they do in order to attract. At a basic level, women are engaged in their lives in order to feel desired and valued by others, including friends, family, and children, but most importantly by a sexual partner. Ultimately, this leads to becoming a parent, which is another primary drive of many women. Competition to find a partner among women is played out by what they wear, their accessories, how beautiful they are, and how much success, power, and resources they can access.

In today's world, women are increasingly demanded to be both feminine and masculine at the same time. They are expected to be the consummate feminine ideal, both inside and out, as well as be able to provide resources and compete professionally with men. This doubles the demands on women, creating stress, pressure, and time scarcity. As a result, women need time and space to take care of themselves more than ever before. Without adequate self-care, it is difficult to feel attractive or desirable.

The primary desire for the man is to be admired. Men are hard-wired to be providers and protectors. They will go all the way to the ends of the earth in order to have someone who appreciates and admires them. Just a little bit of daily admiration towards a man will keep him going for miles. He will bend over backwards to try to please his partner even more if she expresses appreciation for him. When you make a man feel strong and competent through your words and actions, he will thrive, and your relationship will flourish.

I have seen many couples in my practice with sexual issues. In some relationships, sex was good at the beginning and that has never changed. In this type of relationship, the couple is blessed; sex may be the one constant that holds the relationship together through thick and thin. Sex can do a lot to sustain the relational bond between two people. It is one way of connecting intimately when all else fails.

In other couples, sex may have been good in the beginning, but then things changed and it diminished over time. This is sometimes the case after the birth of children, when they become the first priority of the mother. In these relationships, sexual connection can be re-established after the primary focus shifts from the newborn back to the relationship. This is often possible, but both parties need to stay in meaningful communication with one other and actively involved in their own couple relationship outside of parenting. Make the well-being of the couple primary, and the whole family will benefit.

In other relationships, sex was not so great in the beginning, but then it got better. In these evolving relationships, both partners grow together, and the sexual intimacy steadily deepens over time. This is seen in couples who are basically a good match, but did not know each other very well when they made a commitment to each other. Sometimes, you know that you are right for each other even before you really know each other. This is when our unconscious is operating in full force. There are powerful connections that we can experience beyond the conscious level that draw us to one another. If you stay together and keep working on your relationship at all levels, your sexual life can evolve beautifully.

Among the most difficult couples cases that I have worked with are relationships where there was never any chemistry to begin with, but everything else seemed to line up, so both people went ahead with the marriage anyway hoping for the best. In the no-chemistry scenario, the partners just felt that it was "time" to get married.

At a certain age or developmental point, many people feel that they are supposed to have accomplished certain life markers, such as marriage and children. It is amazing how many people live life according to a formula based on what they think they are "supposed" to do, as opposed to what really feels authentic to them. They may have told themselves that sex was not all that important after all. They cut a deal with themselves because there was enough else that was good about the relationship, or because they were getting their family's approval, or maybe even because they unconsciously wanted to defy their family.

In a relationship where there is little or no sexual connection, the need for sex does not disappear. It will usually manifest in some way, whether that be some other passion, an affair, or even an addiction of some sort. I have seen many cases of long-term marriages in which one partner has had a secret sexual life, does not want to give up the marriage, and struggles with the guilt of living a double life. Not everyone has the guilt, but the hidden conflict often expresses itself in some other way.

There are also those who have come to terms with the different compartments of their lives, and have learned to live comfortably with having their needs met from different people. It all depends on the individual's value system. It is difficult to create chemistry that does not exist, but it is possible to compromise sexually, be creative, and come to a sexual resting place that is "good enough."

Sometimes, people are tempted to withhold sex when a conflict has arisen but has not been resolved to their satisfaction. It can be a weapon used to punish their partner for not behaving as they would like. This generally leads to further deterioration in the relationship and does not resolve the original issue. It only diminishes the bond and makes matters worse.

Having sex can restore the bond in a relationship so that the issue of conflict can later be discussed and resolved harmoniously. It is difficult to resolve issues while in a broken state and sometimes much wiser to first repair the bond as much as possible and then tackle the sticky issues when you are in a stronger place together. With a restored bond, your relationship will have the strength and resiliency to resolve issues productively.

One fantasy that we need to give up is that of finding the "perfect" mate. There is no perfect partner, sexually or otherwise. When we relinquish fantasy and begin to live in reality, we come to understand that all partners are wonderful in some ways and deficient in others. We may never have all of our sexual needs met or fantasies fulfilled by our partner, but we can enjoy trying.

Communicating and negotiating your sexual needs will improve your relationship. Talk to each other openly and honestly about your specific sexual needs. This may include emotional intimacy as part of your sexuality, as well as physical release. Discussing frequency of sex is also important. If you are both busy people and leave it to chance, it may not happen very often. Sometimes, couples schedule sex into their life just as they would any other important appointment. Try to have sex at least once a week, if possible.

Use it or lose it. If you are physically able, I recommend having sex regularly whether you are in the mood or not. If both partners have healthy sexual functioning, it is essential to keep your sexuality alive. You may often find that the mood comes upon you once you physically bring yourself to the situation. Waiting for the mood to strike can leave you vulnerable to a multitude of distractions, as well as your sexual relationship losing its priority. Just as we need to give our bodies physical exercise whether we feel like it or not, it is vital to the health of your relationship bond to have a physical relationship. Even if you are are unable to have sex, physical contact with your partner releases powerful bonding hormones that keep a couple connected. It is important to understand each other's needs for enjoyment and fulfillment. Your physical relationship can be one of the most mutually gratifying aspects of your relationship.

It is up to us to make the most of our relationship. You won't have each other forever, even if it feels like you will. Learn how to have fun and play together. Keep flirting with each other; don't take each other for granted. Just because we get older does not mean that we have to lose the lover within us or the lover next to us. The part of us that craves romance, lust, attraction, and eros can stay alive throughout our entire relationship.

7

MONEY

I have noticed that money is one of the hardest things for people to talk about. They will often talk about their sex lives long before they feel comfortable discussing their finances. Things can get touchy where money is concerned. Money is one of the most common problem issues between partners in couples' therapy. It represents different things to different people. What does money mean to you? It can represent freedom, safety, control, success, security, and self-esteem. For some, it does not mean very much at all, aside from the fact that you need enough of it to pay the bills.

Every couple has their own unique way of dealing with money. For some, there is a total merging of finances. For others, money is kept completely separate between partners. There are a multitude of compromise arrangements that work for everyone, depending on how they fit with each person's needs, wants, and financial picture.

The time of life when a couple gets together plays a significant role in the negotiation of financial arrangements. A young couple who begins their adult life together and builds assets together is much more likely to share assets and finances than a newly formed middle aged or older couple who come into the relationship with their own significant assets. People who have accumulated wealth prior to a later marriage often seek prenuptial or postnuptial agreements to clarify the disposition of assets in the event of death or divorce.

When one partner has assets at the beginning of a relationship and the other partner does not, finances are inherently imbalanced, but the relationship may balance out in some other way. There are many ways to contribute in a relationship, including through parenting of the children. Parenting may well be one of the most difficult jobs around, and it commands enormous respect. As a full-time parent, you are almost never off. It is a twenty-four hour a day job, and if done well, one of the most important functions in our society.

When there have been real estate and children from previous marriages factored into the financial equation, the possibilities expand further. If you both have children from previous marriages, finances are often merged to some degree to attend to current expenses, and other assets are often left to one's own heirs or to the surviving spouse. It is essential to have a very clear understanding about your estates so that both partners have peace of mind and no one is surprised at the eleventh hour.

Couples have varying involvement with previous families and children. I have seen some couples who financially treat their stepchildren as their own children, and others who barely have any personal or financial relationship with them at all. The relationship itself usually determines the finances, not rules or norms about family. In current times, the rules for families have changed enormously, as the nature of what defines a family has evolved to the point where there are fewer rules or norms than ever before.

Money is one of the arenas where our control issues are played out. If you had a parent who controlled you with money, the roots of this can run very deep. Money may have represented power, authority, or safety. We often seek a sense of security in money, hoping that if we have enough of it, we will be safe from the perils of life. While we do need enough to live well, at a certain point, more money does not really improve the quality of our lives. But you have to get to the point where you have enough to realize that. That pursuit can easily take up the first half of your life.

If both partners in a couple earn their own money, the relationship is fairly autonomous on both sides, and the power struggle over money is minimal. Both partners generally feel that they have the freedom to do what they want to do with their money as well as contribute their fair share to the couples' expenses.

In other cases, one partner may not feel the need for their own money. In this case, they are financially dependent on the other partner, but may contribute to their lives together in other ways. This could be through childcare responsibilities, home management, or through service to the other partner. Sometimes the dependent partner has not yet developed his own career and has no choice about the matter. It takes a very secure person to allow himself to be financially dependent, as this requires finding a sense of security and self-worth in ways that don't involve money. This dynamic also requires a high level of trust on the part of the dependent partner. It says that the dependent partner trusts the provider to take care of him or her.

Some of us want to be taken care of financially because it makes more logistical sense. For example, if a new mother goes to work and has to pay most of her salary towards childcare while she is at work, it often makes more financial sense for her to just stay home and take care of her children herself.

In other cases, people want to be taken care of financially because they were taken care of by their families and they expect it. They have become accustomed this type of support, and it is part of their model of "how it ought to be." In other cases, people want to be taken care of because they lacked care from their parents and want financial support in order to make up for the deprivation they experienced in childhood. In these cases, the partner is the person who makes up for the deficits of the family-of-origin, and the dependent person has a corrective emotional experience.

The world has changed. One hundred years ago, women did not work as much as they do now. Men used to be the only one working outside of the home. Now that women work, they frequently have their own money and more autonomy over themselves. There is also more to shop for now. We are all addicted to more and more and more in this culture, and the culture itself tells us that we must have more and more things in order to live. There is a constant message that you need to buy something else: something newer, bigger, and better.

This phenomenon feeds into the chronic inherent discomfort that comes from simply being alive. We mistakenly believe that we are supposed to be happy and comfortable all the time, but that is not the reality of life. We are supposed to be uncomfortable at times, and we are not supposed to try to throw money at our feelings in order to medicate them. The ease of shopping online contributes to this phenomenon and can lead to compulsive shopping and getting into debt. If one person in a couple has a different tolerance for debt than the other, there is a potential source of conflict.

Real estate and credit card debt are other areas where couples' value systems and conflicts can play out. One person may have more tolerance for debt and house payments, while the other may not. It is important to discuss these issues prior to making a commitment to someone, otherwise you run the risk of finding yourself in a clash of values and finances. If you marry, that commitment becomes legal and binding, and it can affect your finances for many years.

In general, it is wise to have a reasonable spending plan and to record your expenses, whether your finances are merged or separate. Clarity about finances is what keeps your life manageable and allows you to plan for the future. Working together to create a budget that reflects the needs and priorities of both people will alleviate financial stress. Remember that there is a difference between "needs" and "wants." "Needs" must always come before "wants" in the spending plan.

List all shared and individual income and thoroughly itemize expenditures by category. Major categories include housing, food, transportation, technological communication, education, personal care, medical, household expenses, entertainment, travel, and savings. When there is conflict about how to spend money, try to compromise so that both of you are able to get some of what you want. The objective is to seek a shared vision about financial expenditures and a workable, mutual agreement.

8

FAMILY

In today's world, there are now many configurations known as a "family." We now see conventional marriages with biological children born to both parents, adopted children, step-parents, gay couples, and multiple former marriages with multiple sets of children, with every kind of mix and match combination imaginable.

Family is what you decide it is for yourself. For some, biological family is the only form of family with personal meaning. For others, their family of choice is their true family, and their biological family is just relatives with whom they have little true connection. Being part of a family is a basic human need. We all need a sense of belonging and to feel a part of something greater than ourselves. Humans have a primal need for a "tribe." Since the ancient times of our hunter-gatherer ancestors, we have had a drive to be with one another, eat together, and tell stories. Although times have changed, our needs remain the same.

In today's world, the family has gradually grown smaller and smaller. We no longer need a huge family to work on the farm or to gather food in order to survive. Especially if we live in cities, we are increasingly isolated and alone. As technology connects us in the virtual world, we see less of one another in the real world.

Although the birth rate has been declining in our culture as many people choose to live "childfree" lives, many others still choose to have their own family. This can mean having children, adopting children, step-parenting, foster-parenting, or simply finding people to love. Whether you have actually given birth to a child in your family constellation is not as important as having people to love in your life. Whether we give birth or not, we all have many opportunities to parent and contribute to the lives of others. What is important is to find a way to positively impact the lives of other people, and to make a difference in the larger world.

If you and your partner decide to have children, your lives will change forever. You will be bound together into eternity through the birth of your children. While children have primary importance in the family soon after birth, it is essential to keep your relationship with your partner in first place in the long run. Your relationship will sustain both of you in a way that nothing else can. It needs time, attention, care, and priority in order to survive and thrive.

Guard against over-parenting at the expense of your relationship. Our culture has become so child-centric that parents often have no time for a life of their own. They are so busy driving their children from activity to activity and ensuring that they are entertained during every waking moment that children are growing up expecting to be the center of the universe. Put your relationship above being parents. You were a couple first, and this part of your life needs to continue to be nurtured in order to remain intact.

If you have a conflict, try not to argue in from of the children. Take the time to negotiate parenting practices including disciplinary actions, rewards, and home policies in private. Children will often try to split their parents. They will try to get one parent, the softie, to take their side, while the other parent becomes the taskmaster.

Although it is tempting to win favor from your children, it is better to send the message that you cannot be played against your spouse, manipulated or won over by your children. Children can be very clever at trying to get their way. That is their job. They will test the limits. Your job is to set the limits together, and then consistently stick to them. It is best to present a united front to your children whenever possible.

If you are a step-parent, align yourself whenever possible with both the child and their biological parent. Establish your own relationship with the child. Remember their birthdays and special occasions. Don't try to be their parent; they already have one. Avoid any criticism of their biological parent. Remember that the child is one half of that person, and will internalize any negative comments. This is particularly difficult for a child who has been through a divorce, because they can be fragmented and searching for an identity anyway. To the extent that unconditional positive regard can be practiced, it is helpful for everyone.

Even if you don't have biological or step children together, there are still many other ways to parent. You can work together for a mighty cause that will leave the world a better place. You can give birth to creative projects that will impact the world. You can also become actively involved in your own community and with people in your area. Our own communities are full of people who are suffering and need our love.

Embrace each other's friends and family as your own, including ex-spouses, ex-significant others, and anybody else that your partner has deemed important. If someone means enough to your partner to stay in their life, try to accept it and do not let your insecurities get in the way of your bond together. Remember that your partner chose you, not the other person. There is no competition because you have already won.

Through your partnership, you have the capacity to be a force for good for one another's families. You can do a lot of good for your partner's family because you are more neutral about them and don't have as much emotional baggage as you do with your own family. You will be able to see issues from an unbiased perspective, with clarity, healthy detachment, and unconditional love.

9

ACCEPTANCE

Acceptance of each other means that we no longer try to change the other person. There might still be things that we would like to change, but we have given up trying to make the other person be or do anything differently. We know our partner inside and out, we have tried everything under the sun to get them to change, and realize that we will just not get our way about certain things. We know that what we have is better than anything else out there for us. And we accept that.

In my practice, some of my patients seek help because they feel that they no longer love their partners but do not want to end the relationship. While it is possible that through many years of chronic neglect relationships can deteriorate, you don't have to let it get to that point. It is possible to intervene before it feels hopeless.

When you say that you no longer love your partner, what you are really saying is that you have not made a decision to continue to love them and that you don't have the maturity to accept them unconditionally. Love is a decision, not a feeling. Making a decision to love your partner is up to you; your partner cannot give that to you or take it away from you. It is up to you to choose to love and to accept others as they are.

We often come into our relationships with a model of how it should work. One person should do certain things and behave a particular way, while the other person should play another role that we expect them to play. This can be based on what we saw in our families-of-origin or on what we have experienced in our previous relationships. Get rid of your old model of how it ought to be. There is no one model that works for everyone. Each relationship is entirely unique, and the pieces fit together differently. Relationships are all about the fit, not about doing it "right."

In healthy, lasting, and workable relationships we learn to live with partial fulfillment. This means that we can have part of what we want from every relationship, but not all of what we want. This is a reality in all of our relationships, even with our parents and children. We must learn to accept and be grateful for the part that we want, and live with the things we dislike by not focusing on them. We cannot have everything exactly the way we want it. If someone brings enough good into our lives, there is no reason to discard them just because we cannot have it all.

Resentment can creep into a relationship when we feel slighted by our partner. It is vital to forgive over and over and over again. Forgiveness is the highest form of love and acceptance. It is possible to forgive someone for something you despise, even though you do not approve of what they did. If you accept it, you can forgive it. Acceptance does not mean approval; it only means that you accept the reality of what happened, and that you want to move on from the pain. Forgiveness sets you free to move on and releases you from the chains of bitterness. Without forgiveness, we get stuck in negativity, and this keeps us from moving forward in our lives. Overlook the things that you don't like, and focus on the good. What you focus on will grow in your mind.

It is natural to sometimes think about divorce in a long-term relationship. We need to weigh our options at different points in time in a long-term relationship in order to make sure that we really are where we want to be. Thinking about divorce is not the same thing as doing it. When you are in the acceptance stage of a relationship you will think of divorce less often. Most of the time, you will know that this is where you are meant to be. You are committed, have resolved much of your ambivalence, and have made a decision to stay.

Emotional reactivity will diminish. Instead of being controlled by momentary feelings and desires, you will view the big picture of your life, not momentary situations. You know that feelings are not facts and that they will pass. All of them – the good, the bad, and everything in between – will all pass. There is no reason to make impulsive or hasty decisions based on how you feel at the moment. You have been here a thousand times before, and have learned from past experience. You know how to respond slowly and gently as a mature person, instead of reacting quickly like a child. You now have a new model of "how it ought to be" based on the way it really is and what works in your relationship.

While you may not have been the best fit in the beginning, you have learned about each other and have developed the capacity to adapt to each other's vulnerable areas. We all have unresolved childhood wounds, and these are the areas that can create problems in our relationships. When we discover our partner's wounds, we are often surprised that they are not perfect. If we ourselves are not perfect, why would they be perfect? Accepting each other's imperfections frees us from having to be perfect ourselves, and opens the door for us to grow in our capacity to love. Loving the lovable is easy, but loving the unlovable is a more substantial test of our growth capacity for love.

Discover the other person's wounds and try to nurture them. For instance, if you know that your partner has abandonment anxiety and gets anxious when you leave to go on a trip, make an effort to bond closely before you leave, to stay connected during the trip, and then to re-bond when you return. Instead of making your partner feel deficient for having an area of difficulty, make an extra effort to soothe them. This can lead to healing of your partner's original wound and a strengthening of your relationship.

Part of the reason that we are in relationship in the first place is to help to heal our childhood wounds. By re-experiencing our old wounds and then experiencing different responses from ourselves and from others, our wounds can be healed. Even if they are not completely healed, there can be substantial improvement to the point that we hardly even notice them anymore.

Along with respecting each other's vulnerabilities, we also need to accept and respect each other's different needs. For example, some people need a lot of contact and cannot feel secure and attached without it. Other people need a lot of space and time alone and feel engulfed by too much contact. Ironically, these two opposites tend to attract one another, perhaps because nature wants us to find balance through each another.

We all need time and space to grow together, as well as time apart, in order to grow individually. Since you cannot make your partner become like you, accept that they have different needs, and give them what they want as much as you possibly can. Accept that although you may never be the same, you both are able to give each other something that the other one needs in order to heal and grow.

It has always amazed me, after meeting a patient's spouse, how different they can be from their partner. If you want to know what someone's spouse is like, just imagine their opposite. We seem to be brought together with people who are unlike us in order to develop parts of our personality that are lacking. Thank God that your partner is different from you. Would you really want to be with another you?

Another aspect of relationships that we must accept is that a relationship will not remove our basic human sense of existential loneliness. While a healthy relationship does alleviate some of our loneliness, there is a certain amount of loneliness that is part of the human condition. No relationship and no perfect person can make it go away completely. We have to learn to live with it. This is one of the most difficult realities that people face.

People often feel that if they still have any sense of loneliness, then there must be something wrong with their relationship. This is not necessarily the case. They often try to trade in their relationship for another one, hoping that they will not feel any loneliness in the next one, yet the feeling persists. Ultimately, it is an inside job. We must all accept the responsibility for coming to terms with this aspect of our humanity and find constructive ways of doing so.

One of the most powerful ways of dealing with our existential loneliness is through some form of a spiritual life. We need something to hold on to in our lives that can't leave us, die, or make us feel betrayed or abandoned. If we believe in something spiritual that is greater than ourselves, we have an anchor that allows us to live more abundantly in our relationships.

We will not expect people to be more than they possibly can if we have a spiritual anchor that we place above everything and everyone else. If we place our dependence upon something that cannot fail us, we can allow others to be exactly who they are, accept them, and be grateful for what they bring to our lives. In acceptance, we accept the pain that persists in our life, and also make the best of what we have.

In an intimate relationship, we all want to be loved and accepted for who we are, regardless of where we are on our path. When we truly accept others and our lives as they are, we experience more gratitude. Gratitude, a by-product of acceptance, is the magic key to living a positive, abundant, and productive life. It draws more positive people and experiences towards you, and allows you to overlook the negative. Try to express appreciation to your partner every single day, even for the small things. You will be amazed at the miraculous transformation that can occur in your relationship.

In the stage of acceptance, we come to terms with who we are, who our partner is, and the perfect imperfection of it all. This is when peace begins. When you reach the stage of acceptance, you realize that nobody is going anywhere. Even though you may have thought about it a million times, you have never actually left. Time and time again you have made the decision to give it a little longer. By default, this is the life you have chosen, and this is the life you have. There is no amount of wishing that can change a shared history. One you have a shared history, it can be difficult to walk away. The longer you stay, the more the relationship becomes part of you. The pieces begin to fit together in a new way that works better than anything you could have ever imagined.

10

INTIMACY

After staying together with our significant others for a period of time and working through issues together, we start to move into true intimacy. This is an ongoing deepening process that occurs in the deepest parts of our being: emotionally, physically, and spiritually. When you have intimacy, there is a feeling of comfort that you experience just through one another's presence.

One essential component of intimacy is to take the time to listen to your partner. Really listen. Try to stop, focus, and give your full attention to your partner. If they feel like you are not listening, they will shut down and stop trying to connect with you. Try to make eye contact and convey that you hear what they are saying, even if you have a different opinion. You can still validate each other's reality. Even if you don't agree, just saying "I hear you" fosters intimacy.

There will be times when your partner needs to talk about something that you have absolutely no interest in. Pretend that you are interested, and allow your partner to say whatever they need to say about it. Part of intimate friendship involves processing what is going on in your head. Your partner might just need you to be a sounding board instead of having a solution. At times, it is better to feign interest even when you don't really care about something in order to allow your partner to talk. You can look like you are interested even if you are not. It is a loving act to take interest in what matters to someone else. It is a way of giving to the other person and to the relationship.

Equally important is the art of communicating. There is a difference between simply talking and really communicating. Many people talk all day long without really saying anything. Make sure that when you speak, you are really saying something of value. Be mindful of your words. Choose them wisely, and make the effort to say what needs to be said, even if it takes courage to do it. Sometimes we talk about certain things we are comfortable talking about, but ignore other issues that really need to be discussed.

Learn to be emotionally vulnerable. It is extremely important to be able to identify what you are feeling, and then communicate that to your partner. Especially in a conflict or difference of opinion, you need to be in touch with what you really feel about the situation. It can sometimes be useful to say, "When you do X, I feel Y, and what I need from you is Z." By focusing on your own feelings, instead of what the other person did, you are less likely to experience defensiveness or stonewalling from your partner and can begin a productive conversation.

Try to ask people for what you want. Just because someone loves you does not mean that they can read your mind or know everything about how you feel. You set others up for failure when you expect them to read your mind. You also set yourself up to be an immature victim when you do not take responsibility for your own feelings and ask for what you want. Remember that asking is not the same as demanding. You can make the request, but you have no control over the outcome. Making the request is often good enough to increase your sense of self-esteem in the situation, regardless of whether or not your request is met.

Intimacy also involves learning how to play together. As adults, we still need to play. Most of us are still little kids at heart. We get older and bigger, but we really don't change all that much. We all need to be able to relax and have fun. If your partner can also be your playmate, you will enjoy each other to no end. Learn about what is fun for each other, and try to do some of each person's preferred activities. You may learn how to have fun in creative ways that you never thought possible.

Another one of the keys to sustaining intimacy is respect. We often show respect to those we hardly know, but forget to respect the people we love the most. It is important to practice good behavior when no one else is looking, when we are not trying to impress anyone. We do this because this is who we want to be. It reflects an authentic core of integrity.

Give encouragement to your partner whenever possible. We spend much of our time out in the world operating alone. Your intimacy will thrive if you support one another in individual passions, for example, sports, travel, or hobbies. If your partner likes to travel, and you are not crazy about it, be adventurous, compromise, and try to share his or her passions. Our partner will often enlarge our lives in ways that we could not do alone. That is one of the reasons that our partner is in our life.

While your relationship with your partner may be the most important relationship in your life, it should not be the only relationship in your life. Supporting each other's outside relationships adds to your relationship in that it creates more balance in both of your lives and spreads out each person's dependency needs among different people. No one person, not even the most perfect partner, can meet all of your needs. You are the person who is responsible for meeting your own needs through a variety of people and resources. This means having a diversity of relationships in your life.

In an unhealthy codependent dynamic, both people become the center of each other's lives to an unhealthy degree. They lose themselves in the relationship and experience a self-abandonment that places unrealistic and unsustainable demands upon the primary relationship. While healthy intimate relationships are interdependent, they are not codependent. Each person has a healthy sense of themself, their own life, their own activities, and their outside relationships. Both partners have healthy boundaries, know their own limitations in the relationship: where they end and where the other person begins.

One of the most overlooked aspects of intimacy is kindness. We remember to be kind to strangers, but forget to be kind to the people closest to us. We take each other for granted, and expect that our significant other will always be there, regardless of how we treat them. Simple kindness goes a long way towards sustaining intimacy, emotional safety, and closeness. If you find yourself being unkind, do a self-care check, and ask yourself if there is an area of your life where you are neglecting to take care of yourself. If so, give a little more to yourself, and then your capacity for kindness will return.

Supporting one another emotionally is a hallmark of intimacy. This can mean listening, talking, or just giving each other time and space. Giving each other silence and space can be incredibly loving and healing. Solitude is essential for emotional and spiritual balance in our lives. There is a difference between loneliness and solitude; loneliness is about isolation and disconnection, while solitude is about connecting with ourselves and with God. Silent companionship that requires nothing from you can be very intimate. Being able to do this may require you to tolerate your own anxiety and temporarily put your own needs aside for the benefit of the relationship.

There is a time for everything, and your turn will come.

Take the risk to honestly share your dreams and visions with your partner. You both may have individual as well as shared visions for your life. If you have different goals, stand behind one another as long as the relationship is not hurt, even if you don't always agree. When you have the support of a partner behind you, your dreams can become reality far more easily. There is only so much we can do by ourselves, but with each other and wraparound support, our capacities expand exponentially.

Give your partner your best self. This means making an effort in every area of your relationship, whether you want to or not, including making an effort to look good, to speak well, and to not make a habit of complaining. When our relationships are new, we tend to put our best foot forward. We relax and stop trying so hard to be at our best when we know that the other person is not going anywhere. Pretty soon, we can become complacent and sloppy in our primary relationship, de-prioritizing the most important person in our life. This spirit of complacency is the beginning of the end. Instead, try to remain grateful, and give your partner your best.

This begins with the regular practice of gratitude. Give thanks at every opportunity, for small and big things. There are many more opportunities with small things; you can express appreciation every single day. The more that you operate with a grateful attitude, the happier you will feel, and the healthier your relationship will be. A deep and loving long-term relationship based in gratitude and friendship will thrive.

True intimacy is based in friendship and in being each other's best friend. This can be achieved only when we have grown up enough to be okay by ourselves as well as in a relationship. If you are always looking for someone to complete you, it is difficult to have healthy intimacy. In a healthy relationship, intimacy will continue to grow over time. It is truly about being each other's best friend and wanting to grow old with the person you love the most.

11

LOVE

Love is the foundation of your relationship. The highest form of spiritual development is our capacity to love. Our relationships are our greatest teacher is this lifelong art. Many people feel that true love is based on their own feelings. Their expectation is that when they have true love, they will intensely love another over time and that it will feed them what they need. This is partially true, but there is much more. True love is not dependent on the person being loved, but on the lover him or herself.

True love is about your own ability to love another, through all seasons of life, regardless of how you think they make you feel. It is a decision, not a feeling. When you make a true decision to love, nothing can change your mind. You have made a commitment to practice loving behavior, no matter what. Nothing that you do, or that the other person does, will make you stop loving them. Even if they ultimately leave your life for some reason, you still love them.

Most people think that love is something that they either feel or don't feel. Love is an action, not a feeling. The highest form of love is unconditional love. This means that your spirit is steadfast and persevering, regardless of what the other person does or does not do. You love does not depend on them. It depends on you. We love people not because of who they are, but because of who we are. We make an effort to extend ourselves in order to meet their needs and enhance their well-being.

This may involve stretching beyond your own comfort zone for the welfare of someone you love. The action of love results in someone else feeling better about his or her own life and situation.

We can love others unconditionally and do loving things even if we don't like them at the moment. We can make a decision to develop a loving character and to live according to the values that we choose and not by our feelings. Agape love is unconditional love, which equals character. It comes from a pure heart, a clear conscience, and faith. It is the highest form of love and character development and means that the love is unconditional and unending. Agape love is what we feel from God. It brings us into mature love.

As a relationship deepens, mature love evolves. Regardless of our ages, we have grown up together. It is never too late to grow up emotionally and psychologically. At this stage, we are together because we want to be together, not because we need something from each other. There is a melding of our souls; we have been knitted together through years of shared history and experience. Like the vibrant colors of a beautiful and colorful tapestry, our lives reflect all the colors of the rainbow. We could not have done without any of the threads, even the dark ones. Each thread of our experience makes the rich tapestry even stronger and more beautiful.

We have made a decision to make the relationship work, no matter what. This means that we will do whatever it takes, for as long as it takes, and we will not waver in our commitment to one another. Our two souls have truly become one. We could no more leave the relationship than cut off one of our arms. It just is not an option. This is the true meaning of "until death do us part." There is a deep faith that we are meant to be together, and that we are indeed an unchanging family in the truest sense of the word.

As younger souls, we were controlled by our emotions. If we felt a feeling, it often automatically determined our behavior and course of action. For example, if something triggered anger in us, we could not stop ourselves from expressing it. We simply had to let it out and have our way. There was an impulsive quality about our nature that controlled us. If we could not arrange life to suit ourselves, we would often take revenge or pout. If we had an unmet desire, we simply could not let it go or delay gratification until a later time. Our selfishness ruled us, and therefore we could not easily live above our feelings and make loving choices towards others or even in our own best interest.

When challenged, love always finds a way. If you are struggling or feeling as though you are unable to love, try to love anyway. Just taking the slightest loving action will change your spirit. There is no action too small to begin the change. Once you begin to behave in a loving way, even though you may not yet feel it inside, you will shift from the negative towards the positive, and you will feel better. Doing something small is better than doing nothing at all. It is not anger that kills relationships as much as indifference. The opposite of love is not hate; it is indifference. Indifference finds excuses, does nothing at all, and a relationship slowly dies.

In maturity, we are able to live above our emotions, delay gratification, and behave in a loving manner even when we don't feel that way. We learn that it will not kill us to not get our own way. In fact, sometimes, things even work out better that way. What we think we want is not always for the best. We learn that delaying gratification can make it all the sweeter in the end. It becomes possible, and even preferable, to conduct ourselves with love regardless of what our partner does. We find that we feel better about ourselves, our spiritual strength deepens, and our self-esteem soars.

There is wisdom in practicing new behavior that we wish to cultivate as part of our character. By practicing new behavior, we begin to experience the fruits of maturity. If we practice respectful behavior over and over again, we will eventually become respectful. This means that we practice listening, not judging, criticizing, and validating the other person's reality. If we practice being kind over and over again, we will become a kinder person. By practicing patience, we cultivate the ability to be patient. Life situations will provide ample opportunities for us to practice new behaviors; it is up to us to make a decision to behave differently. Our feelings will follow along. Eventually, our character will transform.

Another aspect of mature love is to love your partner in ways that make them feel loved, not just in ways that you want to love them. For example, if you like to express your love by preparing a delicious meal, but your partner does not feel loved by that, try to learn and understand what makes your partner feel loved. Perhaps your partner feels more loved by spending time in quality conversation and connecting emotionally. We are all wired differently in terms of what makes us feel loved.

Much of our love language stems from early life experiences that preceded the relationship. It is important to really communicate with one another to understand the deeper aspects of what drives us and makes us tick. It is not just about how you want to express love; it is about how the other person can feel it from you.

Learn to listen to the unspoken ways that your partner expresses love for you. Your partner may be taking care of you instead of manifesting traditionally romantic expressions of love. Your partner may routinely do things for you that reflect love, but you do not even recognize them because you are looking for something else. Don't miss your partner's love, only to recognize it when it is no longer there. Sometimes, love is expressed in practical ways, like taking care of small things that make your life run smoothly. Learn to appreciate every little thing.

One of the most important keys to a successful long-term relationship is not in finding the right person; it is about loving the person you have found. Ask yourself what you have learned about love from your partner. If you are making progress in learning how to love, and focusing more on what you can give, you are moving in the right direction. It is not about what we are getting as it is about what we are giving.

One of the hallmarks of a mature relationship is the desire and ability to give. This comes from a place deep within that is founded in unconditional love. In this type of love, which is similar to the love we feel from God, there are no conditions on loving and giving. We seek to give because we want to, not because we feel that we are supposed to. We give because we have an authentic desire to do so. We have experienced a transformation of the spirit. It becomes part of our character. We have evolved from being selfish, small-minded, immature children to people able to practice the art of loving. We give in order to make our partner feel loved, even when we don't feel like we have very much to give or that we want to. It comes spontaneously from our soul.

We find that although we do not give selfishly in order to get back, that is exactly what happens. There is a principle of mirroring in relationships, in which we tend to get back exactly what we put forth. When we extend positive energy towards others, they do the same in return towards us. The same applies to negative energy. When we are intolerant or fault-finding, we receive the same. What we give to others, they tend to want to give back to us. In the end, we will receive much more love if we are focused on giving love. What we emphasize will always grow, so it is vital to pay attention to our focus.

We have learned to put self aside, when appropriate, and consider the other person's needs equally on a regular basis. Whenever a difficulty arises, we have learned that the solution is always to do the next loving thing. There is a basic trust that has been established and that has solidified over time. We usually know what to expect of one another, yet we are still surprised from time to time. We find the other person interesting and exciting, yet comfortable and predictable in the ways that matter. At this stage, we have never had it so good.

12

GROWTH

The person you are partnered with has been chosen for you and brought into your life for a purpose. Both of you are together to learn from one another, to grow, and to produce something of value. We tend to think that we are in relationships just for ourselves, but this is not really the case. There is more to life than just enjoying ourselves and gratifying our own desires. A healthy relationship is a force multiplier that allows each person to contribute, both individually and together, to the world at a much higher level than they could if they were solo.

At the beginning of a relationship, we tend to partner up with people at our own level. If we have unresolved issues from childhood, we tend to be drawn to a partner with a similar level of development. When we mature, we are then drawn to others at our new maturity level. If we both make the effort to grow, the relationship is likely to survive. If one person grows and the other does not, there is less chance of longevity for the relationship. One person may be left behind while the other moves beyond them. This is a case when the pieces do not continue to find a new fit together, and one person literally outgrows the other.

If we find ourselves with a partner whom we consider to be difficult to deal with, there may be a reason that we are together. Perhaps we are with this person in order to learn lessons about ourselves that we could not learn any other way. We might not be able to grow without the necessary pain of going through the difficulties that result from the relationship. In God's economy, nothing is wasted. The gift of having a difficult partner is that you must grow or go. If you are truly committed, you will do whatever is necessary in order to grow.

One person may be at a stuck-point due to emotional blocks, addictions, or simply an unwillingness to self-examine dysfunctional patterns due to ego and pride. One of the most important qualities when assessing your choice for a partner is whether or not they are willing to address and deal with their own issues. If they are willing to work on their own issues, you have a good chance of evolving together. Each must do his own work on an ongoing basis.

Ongoing growth occurs when people have resolved the basic issues around commitment, trust, and acceptance, and are now engaged in fine-tuning and furthering their journey. Regular self-examination is a key to constant progress and not getting stuck again. This can be done through reading, writing, discussion, psychotherapy, and support groups.

It is also important to continue in your own spiritual journey. Through an ongoing and sustained effort at spiritual growth, your relationship with God will deepen and lengthen over time. Like any relationship with a human being, your continued relationship with God will continue to grow and evolve into something more and more beautiful, bearing more and more fruit. The spiritual life draws you in ever so gently, always fulfilling you and filling you with awe, wonder, gratitude, and peace.

A relationship is meant to produce something. As you evolve, your relationship, shared values, and the fruits of your partnership can make an impact on the world. Your partnership is a spiritual relationship between both partners and God. Prayer is the action that keeps the communication flowing. I recommend praying together every day in order to access spiritual forces that will help to sustain your relationship as well as increase its fruits. The prayers do not have to be long, and you can just use plain and simple language that you would use when talking to a close friend. Talking to God regularly and staying in communication is what is important.

The fruits of staying together over a long period of time include having the ability to help others to do the same thing, learning how to love and be an example to those who look up to you, and devoting yourself to a cause outside of yourself that gives you a sense of purpose and meaning. You each can contribute much more individually because of the relationship, as you are not spending time and energy trying to medicate your need for companionship or to find a partner. Your relationship is a home base that allows you to go about the world and contribute more fully to other things. It keeps your tank full.

Ultimately, the world can be a better place because you are with your partner. Contributing to the world may involve having children, but is not limited to that. You can help others in many different ways as the result of your own life experience, whatever that may be. It is up to each one of us to discover what is our gift for the world, and then to give it. After finding out who we are and learning how to meet our needs, we then have the opportunity to find out what we are able to contribute in order to leave this world a little bit better than we found it. The life journey is all about contributing and giving something back. This is the true purpose of our lives and our relationships.

ABOUT THE AUTHOR

Dr. Anita Gadhia-Smith, author of three other books, is a psychotherapist in Washington, D.C. specializing in addictions, recovery, and relationship issues. She is particularly effective, discerning and insightful about current issues that have a psychological impact on individuals and couples. She has served as a consultant to the United States Congress in parity legislation for substance abuse treatment. She has also spoken nationally and internationally on radio, television, and other media as an expert on a variety of topical subjects.

One of the things that distinguishes Dr. Anita Gadhia-Smith is her own personal history of addiction as well as over two decades of recovery. She has had a first-hand experience of a spiritual, physical and emotional "bottoming out" followed by a remarkable story of recovery and commitment to helping others who suffer with alcoholism, addictions and relationship issues. Her history and training allow her to approach her work, her perspective and her writing as a "healed healer." Her story is one of redemption – she is a unique therapist who has become a successful, self-actualized woman by way of an intense struggle and personal journey in her own right. Her insights and wisdom are tremendous – and inspiring – about how to obtain and maintain ongoing balance in our lives. Dr. Gadhia-Smith's other bestselling books, "FROM ADDICTION TO RECOVERY," "PRACTICAL THERAPY," AND "LIVE AND LOVE EACH DAY" are available on Amazon. com.

Dr. Gadhia-Smith earned her undergraduate degree from The Johns Hopkins University (BA, 1985) and graduate degrees from The Catholic University of America (MSW, 1999) and Southern California University, (PSYD, 2001). In her private practice in Washington, D.C., Dr. Gadhia-Smith works with adults and adolescents in individual, couple, and family modalities and says, "Therapy is a journey through which we find our authentic selves and become the best we can be. Through therapy, profound and lasting change can occur. My approach is to meet you where you are and to help you to move towards your goals, overcome obstacles and achieve maximum growth."

Awarded "Best of Washington DC, Psychotherapy, 2013" by the Washington DC

Award Program. Honored as Professional of the Year in Psychotherapy by Strathmore's Who's Who Publication, 2013-2014. Visit her website at www.practicaltherapy.net.

CPSIA information can be obtained at www.ICGtesting.com
Printed in the USA
BVOW04s1439021013

332652BV00001B/3/P